gentleness

Other Studies in the Fruit of the Spirit Bible Study Series

gentleness

The Strength of Being Tender

Phyllis J. Le Peau

GRAND RAPIDS, MICHIGAN 49530

ZONDERVAN

Gentleness: The Strength of Being Tender
Copyright © 1991, 2001 by Phyllis J. Le Peau
Requests for information should be addressed to:
Zondervan, *Grand Rapids, Michigan 49530*

ISBN 978-0-310-23864-5

Interior design by Melissa Elenbaas

Printed in the United States of America

CONTENTS

FRUIT OF THE SPIRIT
BIBLE STUDIES

Welcome to Fruit of the Spirit Bible Studies. This series was written with one goal in mind—to allow the Spirit of God to use the Word of God to produce his fruit in your life.

To get the most from this series you need to understand a few basic facts:

Fruit of the Spirit Bible Studies are designed to be flexible. You can use them in your quiet times or for group discussion. They are ideal for Sunday school classes, small groups, or neighborhood Bible studies.

The eight guides in this series can be used in any order that is best for you or your group.

Because each guide contains only six studies, you can easily explore more than one fruit of the Spirit. In a Sunday school class, any two guides can be combined for a quarter (twelve weeks), or the entire series can be covered in a year.

Each study deliberately focuses on only one or two passages. That allows you to see each passage in its context, avoiding the temptation of prooftexting and the frustration of "Bible hopscotch" (jumping from verse to verse). If you would like to look up additional passages, a Bible concordance will give the most help.

The questions help you *discover* what the Bible says rather than simply *telling* you what it says. They encourage you to think and to explore options rather than to merely fill in the blanks with one-word answers.

Leader's notes are provided in the back of the guide. They show how to lead a group discussion, provide additional information on questions, and suggest ways to deal with problems that may come up in the discussion. With such helps, someone with little or no experience can lead an effective study.

SUGGESTIONS FOR INDIVIDUAL STUDY

1. Begin each study with prayer. Ask God to help you understand the passage and to apply it to your life.
2. A good modern translation, such as the *New International Version,* the *New American Standard Bible,* or the *Revised Standard Version,* will give you the most help. However, the questions in this guide are based on the *New International Version.*
3. Read and reread the passage(s). You must know what the passage says before you can understand what it means and how it applies to you.
4. Write your answers in the space provided in the study guide. This will help you to clearly express your understanding of the passage.
5. Keep a Bible dictionary handy. Use it to look up any unfamiliar words, names, or places.

SUGGESTIONS FOR GROUP STUDY

1. Come to the study prepared. Careful preparation will greatly enrich your time in group discussion.
2. Be willing to join in the discussion. The leader of the group will not be lecturing but will encourage people to discuss what they have learned in the passage. Plan to share what God has taught you in your individual study.
3. Stick to the passage being studied. Base your answers on the verses being discussed rather than on outside authorities such as commentaries or your favorite author or speaker.
4. Try to be sensitive to the other members of the group. Listen attentively when they speak, and be affirming whenever you can. This will encourage more hesitant members of the group to participate.
5. Be careful not to dominate the discussion. By all means, participate! But allow others to have equal time.
6. If you are the discussion leader, you will find additional suggestions and helpful ideas in the leader's notes at the back of the guide.

GENTLENESS

The Strength of Being Tender

When Sis Levin's husband, Jerry, was kidnapped by Lebanese terrorists, she remained in Lebanon to seek his release. Instead of hostility, demands, and accusations against the people who held Jerry's life in their hands, she responded in gentleness. She cared for the children of that country and brought music to a cultural center established for them. She loved the people. At the time she was not aware of the strength of her tenderness.

While she was caring for these children, Jerry's normal crusts of bread and small pieces of cheese were suddenly replaced with warm food, fruit, and chocolate. His captors brought him extra socks and blankets. They even asked him what he wanted for a Christmas present. He requested and received a Bible.

Finally, he was allowed to escape. It wasn't until Sis and Jerry were together that Jerry knew why these sudden changes had taken place.

Gentleness is a vital necessity in many of our relationships in life—relationships with people in whom change comes very slowly, if at all. Often, instead of being gentle with them, we are harsh, abrupt, or defensive.

Yet we cannot grit our teeth and make ourselves into gentle people. It is truly a *fruit*. Gentleness can be produced in us only by the Spirit of God. Therefore, we simply and humbly admit our need and search the Scriptures for God's perspective on gentleness.

This Fruit of the Spirit Bible study is for people who, like me, want the fruit of gentleness to grow in them. We will begin by considering the fact that gentleness is not weakness. Next we will explore what it is to be gentle with the weak, with our words, and in our ministry. Finally, we will look at the gentleness of wisdom and the relationship between gentleness and power. I hope you will enjoy discovering more about gentleness, and may we learn together how to experience this vital fruit of the Spirit.

one

GENTLENESS IS NOT WEAKNESS

Matthew 21:1–17

Gentle Jesus, meek and mild, look upon a little child." Jesus is often portrayed as gentle in poems, hymns, and paintings. Yet his "gentleness" seems limp, almost effeminate. His pale, white skin and his delicate features make him seem soft, weak, retiring.

What a contrast to the Jesus of Scripture! In Matthew 21 we discover that there is strength in his gentleness and gentleness in his strength.

Warming Up

1. Why do you think people sometimes assume that a gentle person is also a weak person?

Digging In

2.   Read Matthew 21:1–17. What impact do you think the events in verses 1–11 had on the disciples? On the crowd?

3.   According to verse 5, the prophet Zechariah describes Jesus as *gentle* (Zech. 9:9). How is his gentleness demonstrated in the way he approaches Jerusalem (vv. 5–11)?

4.   There is a sudden change of tone as Jesus enters the temple. What motivates Jesus' actions in verses 12–13?

5. How do Christ's actions in the temple contrast with the popular image of "gentle Jesus, meek and mild"?

6. In what kinds of situations is a firm, tough love more appropriate than a gentle response?

7. How is Christ's gentleness again demonstrated in his response to the blind, the lame, and the children (vv. 14–15)?

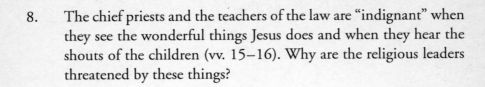

8. The chief priests and the teachers of the law are "indignant" when they see the wonderful things Jesus does and when they hear the shouts of the children (vv. 15–16). Why are the religious leaders threatened by these things?

9. How would you evaluate Christ's response to their challenge (vv. 16–17)? Is he confrontive? Gentle? Both?

10. What do you learn about gentleness as you observe Jesus through-out this passage?

11. In what ways do you struggle to achieve a gentleness that is not weak and a strength that is not harsh?

Pray about It

Ask God to develop the fruit of gentleness within you as you seek to follow the example of Jesus.

TAKING THE NEXT STEP

Based on what you have seen in Matthew 21, write a clear description and definition of gentleness. List the characteristics of Jesus that you see in this passage as preparation for creating this definition. Then reflect upon and jot down situations and relationships in which you would like to see the fruit of gentleness grow in you. For the next week make notes on the ways you are growing in gentleness.

two

BEING GENTLE WITH THE WEAK

Matthew 12:15–21

My friend Pattie is the principal of the school where our children attend. I love to see her discipline children. It both challenges and convicts me. Because most children, by nature, are transparent and vulnerable, they feel weak when they have done something wrong. Even so, when disciplining them my tendency is to be quick, harsh, angry, impatient, frustrated. Pattie is always gentle. She deals with the offense head-on. The children know beyond a doubt the nature of the offense, its consequences, and what will happen in the future if they do it again. But they also know that they are forgiven and loved. Though they have been weak, they leave strengthened by her tenderness.

Warming Up

1.   What common types of weakness do people experience?

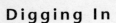

Digging In

2.   Read Matthew 12:15–21. As you read this passage, what are your initial impressions about Jesus?

3.   What do you think it means that "he will not quarrel or cry out; no one will hear his voice in the streets" (v. 19)?

4.   What is it like for you to be around someone who seeks controversy or who proclaims truth in an assertive and abrasive manner?

5. What do a "bruised reed" and a "smoldering wick" represent (v. 20)?

6. How does Jesus respond to each?

7. When have you felt like a reed that was bruised or a wick that was about to go out?

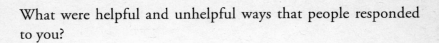

What were helpful and unhelpful ways that people responded to you?

8.   How do you generally respond to those who are physically, emotionally, or spiritually weak?

How would you like to respond?

9.   Proclaiming and promoting justice is an important part of Jesus' ministry (vv. 18, 20). How does gentleness, especially to the weak, contribute to that mission?

Pray about It

Think about a relationship in which you are struggling to be gentle. Ask God's Spirit to develop the fruit of gentleness in you as you grow in that relationship.

TAKING THE NEXT STEP

Create a modern paraphrase of verses 18 to 21. Instead of Jesus being the main character, write it about yourself. Think through specifically how you, as a follower of Jesus, would look if these verses described you. For instance, what would it mean in your life for you to be a servant? To have God's Spirit reigning in you? To proclaim justice to the nations (v. 18)? What would it be like for you to not quarrel or cry out (v. 19)? To respond as he did to the bruised reeds and smoldering wicks in your life?

three

BEING GENTLE WITH OUR WORDS

Proverbs 15:1, 4; 25:15

After twenty-five years of marriage, I am still affected (most of the time) by my husband's gentle response when I am angry. His tender words defuse a potentially explosive situation. In the proverbs we are considering in this study, we will see the power of gentle words.

Warming Up

1.   In what situations do gentle words mean the most to you?

Digging In

2.   Read Proverbs 15:1, 4. Verse 1 states that a gentle answer turns away wrath. When have you experienced this?

3.   When have you seen anger stirred up by harsh words?

4.   According to verse 4, what contrasting effects can a tongue have?

5.   What do you think it means to crush someone's spirit with a deceitful tongue (v. 4)?

6.   It is a sobering fact that our tongues can crush spirits. Can you think of examples when you or someone else crushed another's spirit with words? Explain.

7.   How would you describe a tree of life (v. 4)? What is it like? What does it do?

8.   When has God used your tongue for healing in another's life, or when has someone else's tongue brought you healing?

9.   What steps do you need to take for your tongue to speak words of life more frequently?

10.   Read Proverbs 25:15. What do patience and a gentle tongue have in common?

11. What do you think it means that a gentle tongue can break a bone?

12. How do the proverbs in this study challenge and encourage you about your words?

Pray about It

Confess to the Lord Jesus that sometimes you are not even aware of the effect your words have on others. Ask him to make you sensitive to how you can encourage and heal others with words and to convict you about hurtful and destructive words before you speak them.

TAKING THE NEXT STEP

Memorize and reflect daily on Proverbs 15:4. Consider how your tongue can bring healing to others. Contact at least one person every day to share words of encouragement and affirmation. Pray for that person that God will use your words for healing in his or her life.

four

BEING GENTLE IN OUR MINISTRY

1 Thessalonians 2:1–12

I love babies. We are raising four children. Our oldest is thirteen, and the youngest is seven. We are in a new era—lots of independence and self-sufficiency. A couple of them are even taking care of other people's children. There are *no more babies around.* Even so, I have to admit that this is a fun period in our lives.

There are scenes, however, that still touch me deeply and cause old longings to emerge; for instance, watching a mother nurse her infant or a father teach his toddler how to play catch or kick a soccer ball. What tender pictures of love and nurture! They are precious times of security and contentment for the children and of great satisfaction for Mom and Dad. How appropriate that Paul uses the image of parenting, full of gentleness and nurture, when he describes his spiritual ministry to the Thessalonians.

Warming Up

1.   What gentle moments with your mom and dad do you remember from your childhood?

29

Digging In

2.   Read 1 Thessalonians 2:1–12. What had Paul's visit to Thessalonica been like according to verses 1–2?

3.   How would you describe Paul's motives in ministering to the Thessalonians (vv. 3–6)?

4.   What usually motivates you to share the gospel and nurture other Christians?

5.   In what ways was Paul like a mother to the Thessalonians (vv. 7–9)?

6.   What do you think it meant that he shared not only the gospel with them but his life as well?

7.   In what ways was Paul also like a father to the Thessalonians (vv. 10–12)?

8. When have other Christians treated you with motherly gentleness or fatherly care?

How did you respond to their love and concern?

9. What was the ultimate goal of Paul's ministry (v. 12)?

10. What can you do this week to encourage, comfort, or urge someone to live a life more worthy of God?

How can you express gentleness in your ministry as you aim for that goal?

Pray about It

Thank God for specific people who have encouraged you to live a life worthy of God by gently sharing their lives and the gospel. Ask God to help you to gently share your life and the gospel with others.

TAKING THE NEXT STEP

Journal about the people in your life who have most significantly encouraged and urged you to live a life worthy of God. What characteristics and qualities did they possess? How were you specifically affected by them? How might you affect others for the kingdom by following their examples?

five

THE GENTLENESS OF WISDOM

James 3:13–18

Lord, please give me wisdom," I prayed as Philip and Susan ran to me in tears. Both children had their own story, and they stood before me arguing. Most of the time this type of event frustrates me as I try to get to the truth and take appropriate action. I usually walk away discouraged and defeated.

God's response to my plea came in the form of a plan of action. I calmly sent the children into a room together and told them to come out when their stories agreed. In a short time they came out, agreeing and content. All three of us experienced the gentleness of God's wisdom.

Warming Up

1. What do you think it means to be wise?

Digging In

2.   Read James 3:13–18. According to verse 13, how are wisdom and understanding demonstrated?

3.   What do you think it means to live a "good life"? To be humble?

4.   How is humility an important element of being wise?

5.   What are some characteristics of "earthly" wisdom (vv. 14–15)?

6.   What are the results of this kind of wisdom (v. 16)?

7.   What examples of this "earthly wisdom" and its results have you seen in our culture? In your life?

8.   How is the fruit of gentleness evident in the wisdom that comes from heaven (v. 17)?

9.   In what ways have you seen this kind of wisdom in the lives of some of the people you know?

10.   What is a "harvest of righteousness"?

11.   What aspects of heavenly wisdom do you most need in your life?

12.   What can you do to allow this gentle heavenly wisdom to grow more fully in you?

Pray about It

Praise God for heavenly wisdom—wisdom that by his power can be lived out practically in your life. Ask him to give you this wisdom. Believe that he will do it.

TAKING THE NEXT STEP

Write a letter to God. Tell him about any envy and bitterness you are harboring in your heart. Then write about any selfish ambition you are experiencing. Tell him specifically how you would like for him to replace earthly wisdom with wisdom that is from above. Describe what that would look like in your life. End the letter by thanking him for the harvest of righteousness that he is producing in you.

six

GENTLENESS AND POWER

2 Corinthians 10:1–11

A powerful person can also be a gentle person—as Jesus himself demonstrates. But what about those who are not powerful, who are gentle in temperament as well as action? Are they disqualified from having a powerful impact on others? Must they become more macho in their ministry to be effective?

In 2 Corinthians 10 Paul is criticized by the Corinthians for being "timid," "unimpressive," and poor at public speaking. Instead of defending himself and flexing his muscles, Paul appeals to them "by the meekness and gentleness of Christ." He also shows why the world's power is powerless in spiritual warfare.

Warming Up

1.   What does the world tend to look for in a powerful person?

Digging In

2.   Read 2 Corinthians 10:1–11. How did Paul fail to measure up to the Corinthians' image of a powerful person?

3.   Why do you think he appeals to them "by the meekness and gentleness of Christ" (v. 1)?

4.   What do you think Paul means when he says "we do not wage war as the world does" (v. 3)?

5.   What evidence of spiritual warfare do you see in and around you?

6.   What spiritual weapons can we use to demolish the arguments and pretensions against God?

7.   What does it mean to "take captive every thought to make it obedient to Christ" (v. 5)?

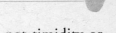

8. How does Paul demonstrate that gentleness is not timidity or weakness (vv. 2, 4–6, 11)?

9. How might you be inclined to defend yourself to someone who said you were "timid" and "unimpressive"?

10. Paul freely admits that his power comes not from himself but from Christ (vv. 4–5, 8). How does this give hope to those who are gentle not only in action but in temperament?

11. In review, what have you learned about the fruit of gentleness in these studies?

Pray about It

Ask God to make this fruit of gentleness increasingly a part of who you are in Christ.

TAKING THE NEXT STEP

In a world that sees power as external, it is difficult to live in "the meekness and gentleness of Christ" (v. 1). One way to experience the power of Christ's gentleness is "to take captive every thought to make it obedient to Christ" (v. 5). Make this your goal throughout the coming week. Journal about specific thoughts you want to take captive and make obedient to Christ. How is your obedience to God affected by being aware of and turning your thought life over to him?

LEADER'S NOTES

Leading a Bible discussion—especially for the first time—can make you feel both nervous and excited. If you are nervous, realize that you are in good company. Many biblical leaders, such as Moses, Joshua, and the apostle Paul, felt nervous and inadequate to lead others (see, for example, 1 Cor. 2:3). Yet God's grace was sufficient for them, just as it will be for you.

Some excitement is also natural. Your leadership is a gift to the others in the group. Keep in mind, however, that other group members also share responsibility for the group. Your role is simply to stimulate discussion by asking questions and encouraging people to respond. The suggestions listed below can help you to be an effective leader.

PREPARING TO LEAD

1. Ask God to help you understand and apply the passage to your own life. Unless that happens, you will not be prepared to lead others.
2. Carefully work through each question in the study guide. Meditate and reflect on the passage as you formulate your answers.
3. Familiarize yourself with the leader's notes for the study. These will help you understand the purpose of the study and will provide valuable information about the questions in the study.
4. Pray for the various members of the group. Ask God to use these studies to bring about greater spiritual fruit in the life of each person.

5. Before the first meeting, make sure each person has a study guide. Encourage them to prepare beforehand for each study.

LEADING THE STUDY

1. Begin the study on time. If people realize that the study begins on schedule, they will work harder to arrive on time.
2. At the beginning of your first time together, explain that these studies are designed to be discussions not lectures. Encourage everyone to participate, but realize that some may be hesitant to speak during the first few sessions.
3. Read the introductory paragraph at the beginning of the discussion. This will orient the group to the passage being studied.
4. Read the passage aloud. You may choose to do this yourself, or you might ask for volunteers.
5. The questions in the guide are designed to be used just as they are written. If you wish, you may simply read each one aloud to the group. Or you may prefer to express them in your own words. However, unnecessary rewording of the questions is not recommended.
6. Don't be afraid of silence. People in the group may need time to think before responding.
7. Avoid answering your own questions. If necessary, rephrase a question until it is clearly understood. Even an eager group will quickly become passive and silent if they think the leader will do most of the talking.
8. Encourage more than one answer to each question. Ask, "What do the rest of you think?" or "Anyone else?" until several people have had a chance to respond.
9. Try to be affirming whenever possible. Let people know you appreciate their insights into the passage.
10. Never reject an answer. If it is clearly wrong, ask, "Which verse led you to that conclusion?" Or let the group handle the problem by asking them what they think about the question.
11. Avoid going off on tangents. If people wander off course, gently bring them back to the passage being considered.

12. Conclude your time together with conversational prayer. Ask God to help you apply those things that you learned in the study.

13. End on time. This will be easier if you control the pace of the discussion by not spending too much time on some questions or too little on others.

Many more suggestions and helps are found in the book *Leading Bible Discussions* (InterVarsity Press). Reading that would be well worth your time.

Study 1

GENTLENESS IS NOT WEAKNESS

Matthew 21:1–17

Purpose: To observe the fact that Jesus is both gentle and strong in his relationships with others.

Question 1. Every study begins with an "approach question," which is discussed *before* reading the passage. An approach question is designed to do three things.

First, it helps to break the ice. Because an approach question doesn't require any knowledge of the passage or any special preparation, it can get people talking and can help them to warm up to each other.

Second, an approach question can motivate people to study the passage at hand. At the beginning of the study, people in the group aren't necessarily ready to jump into the world of the Bible. Their minds may be on other things (their kids, a problem at work, an upcoming meeting) that have nothing to do with the study. An approach question can capture their interest and draw them into the discussion by raising important issues related to the study. The question becomes a bridge between their personal lives and the answers found in Scripture.

Third, a good approach question can reveal where people's thoughts or feelings need to be transformed by Scripture. That is why it is important to ask the approach question *before* reading the passage. The passage might inhibit the spontaneous, honest answers people might have given, because they feel compelled to give biblical answers. The approach question allows them to compare their personal thoughts and feelings with what they later discover in Scripture.

You might follow the approach question in this study by asking the group members if they equate gentleness with weakness.

Question 2. Encourage the group to use their imaginations with this question. One creative way of doing so is to ask them to pretend that they are the disciples or members of the crowd. Then rephrase question 2 as follows: "What impact would the events in verses 1–11 have had on you?"

Putting yourself into the situation helps you experience the thoughts and feelings of those who were there. Imagine what it was like for the disciples to go get the donkey and the colt, or for them to see the words of a prophet fulfilled right before their eyes. Be creative!

Question 3. "The idea [of Christ's gentleness] is further elaborated by the description of His advent upon an untamed colt. The allusion to Gn. 49:10, 11 is clear. Judah will produce a mysterious ruler, who is not a worldly conqueror but will maintain his right by peaceful means. The contrast is strongly marked between the ass and the war-horse, the emblems of peace and war respectively. In the Messianic age weapons of destruction will be banished (cf. Is. 2:2–4; Mi. 5:10; Zc. 8:2–23)" (*The New Bible Commentary: Revised* [Grand Rapids, Mich.: Eerdmans, 1970], 795).

"The Galilean crowds acclaim Him as the local prophet, but the whole symbolism of the occasion marks Him out as Messiah and the context of the quotation from Zechariah indicates His world-wide dominion of peace" (*The New Bible Commentary: Revised,* 842).

Question 4. "Merchants and moneychangers set up their booths in the Court of the Gentiles in the Temple, filling it with their wares instead of allowing it to be filled with Gentiles who had come to worship God. The merchants sold sacrificial animals at high prices, taking advantage of those who had come long distances. The moneychangers exchanged all secular currency for Temple currency—the only kind of money the merchants would accept. They often deceived foreigners who didn't know the exchange rate. Not only were the merchants and moneychangers dishonest; they also took advantage of those who had come to worship God. Their commercialism in God's house frustrated people's attempts to worship. This, of course, angered Jesus" (*Life Application Bible* [Wheaton, Ill.: Tyndale, 1988], note for Matt. 21:12).

Question 5. To aid in discussing this question, you might ask the group, "What images do the words *gentle Jesus, meek and mild* bring to your mind?" "What is Jesus like in this temple scene?" "How do his actions in the temple contrast with these images?"

The contrast brought out in question 5 is important to the theme of this passage. Jesus' gentleness is evident as he enters the city on a donkey. But his gentleness does not preclude the strength it takes to stand for what is right.

Question 6. Sometimes it is difficult for a group to move from the content and theory of a passage to applying it to their own lives. This is the first question in this study that calls for application. As the leader, you can have a great influence on the group by being ready to discuss how you see the passage applies to you. If the group does not readily share, you can set the pace by going first.

The group can respond to this question by talking about general situations in which firm, tough love is needed or by talking about specific situations in which you saw the need. If the group just shares general situations, attempt to lead them to more personal sharing by asking such questions as, "When have you found the need to be firm and tough?" or, "When have you been in a situation when it would have been inappropriate to respond softly?"

Question 7. The blind and the lame came to Jesus and he healed them. The children continued to praise him and he defended them to the chief priests and accepted their praise. This contrast in behavior models to us the complexity of gentleness and our need for Jesus' wisdom in living out gentleness.

Question 8. The words of the children, which echo those of the crowds (v. 9), come primarily from Psalm 118:25–26. *Son of David* is a messianic title that infuriated the religious leaders, especially since Jesus did works that were fitting for the Messiah. The leaders, therefore, feared that Jesus would win the support of the people and overthrow their religious system.

"The children were still using the words of the crowds without fully understanding them, yet this could not be stopped because it was an expression of praise to God the Creator (cf. Lk 19:39f.; Ps. 8:2). Jesus by

His action and His acceptance of the acclamation of the crowds and the children had presented a direct challenge to the whole established order of things" (*The New Bible Commentary: Revised,* 843).

Questions 10–11. These questions are the heart of what you have studied. Be prepared in the event that the group is not responsive. It is risky to be open with where we need to change or where we struggle. Trust has to build. There are no right or wrong answers. Receive what each person says with gentleness. Be ready to share yourself. Pray for one another.

Study 2

BEING GENTLE WITH THE WEAK

Matthew 12:15–21

Purpose: To observe what it is to be gentle with the weak and to seek to become more like that in our relationships with others.

Question 2. "Matthew . . . interprets Jesus' healing ministry, not so much in terms of 'Son of God' or even royal 'Son of David' christology, but in terms of Yahweh's Suffering Servant. This section simultaneously contrasts the hatred of the Pharisees (v. 14) with Jesus' tranquility (v. 19) and gentleness (v. 20)" (D. A. Carson, *Matthew,* The Expositor's Bible Commentary [Grand Rapids, Mich.: Zondervan, 1984], 285).

Question 3. "*He will not wrangle or cry aloud* explains that Jesus did not seek controversy, though He sometimes had to engage in it, and that He did not wish to publish His Messiahship in the wrong way" (*The New Bible Commentary: Revised,* 832).

Question 5. D. A. Carson explains these images as follows: "The double metaphor breathes compassion: the servant does not advance his ministry with such callousness to the weak that he breaks the bruised reed or snuffs out the smoldering wick (smoldering either because it is poorly trimmed or low on oil). This may include reference to Jesus' attitude to the sick (v. 15). But the last clause of v. 20 ('till he leads justice to victory') . . . suggests something more—namely that he brings eschatological salvation to the 'harassed and helpless' (9:36), the 'weary and burdened' (11:28)" (*Matthew,* 286–87).

Question 8. This question may take some effort to answer. For one thing, we do not always respond the same to a person in need. But there are general tendencies. We might feel superior to the person and treat him harshly or with prideful scorn. Or we might feel so sympathetic that we lose both our objectivity and our ability to really help the person. Or we might respond in compassion, feeling genuine concern for the person and expressing that concern in practical ways.

Question 9. "*Brings justice to victory:* the vindication of the ways of God is something seen to be of great importance. This vindication occurs partly through the mission to the outcast and ultimately to the Gentiles" (*The New Bible Commentary: Revised,* 832).

Study 3

BEING GENTLE WITH OUR WORDS

Proverbs 15:1, 4; 25:15

Purpose: To consider the powerful effect of gentle words and to make such words more a part of our everyday speech.

The few verses in this study reveal the power of words in our lives. Throughout this study it is important to allow people the freedom to share the pain they have experienced from others, as well as their own failures and successes with words. Probably more time will be spent in this study on personal experience than in most studies, but such personal time is important to illustrate the truth and the potency of the subject.

Question 1. This question is important for setting the tone. By taking time to think about, share, and feel the power of gentle words, the power of words will be more evident and the pain that comes from words that are misused and destructive will be more intense.

Question 2. Don't be afraid of silence as the members of your group may need some time to think about times in which they have been affected by a gentle answer or have seen it in others. It is an amazing truth that can transform relationships and needs to be thought through and discussed, and steps need to be taken toward responding to others with gentle words.

Question 3. "*A harsh word:* The Hebrew suggests one that hurts. . . . Gentle speech is healing, life giving; twisted speech can crush people" (*The New Bible Commentary: Revised,* 563).

"Single words that hurt is enough to make anger stir up" (Derek Kidner, *Proverbs,* Tyndale Old Testament Commentaries [Downers Grove, Ill.: InterVarsity, 1972], 112).

Question 4. In one short verse both the life-giving and destructive power of words are described. The same tongue that can bring healing can crush the spirit.

Question 5. It is important to allow people the freedom to share the pain they have experienced from others, as well as their own failures and successes with words. In *Making Life Work*, Bill Hybels writes, "I'm sure the reason God detests dishonesty is . . . that it destroys other people. . . .

"Every week at church I meet many people who have had their hearts broken by lies and deceit and twisted truths . . . spirits crushed by dishonesty and deceit. . . .

"In many cases, if you trace their disappointment back far enough you discover a trail of dishonesty. It may have started with a slight departure from the point of absolute truthfulness, but all too often that first dishonest step leads to deeper forms of deceitfulness and from there to flat-out lies. . . .

"Have you told any lies lately? Any 'harmless' little half-truths? 'We'll do lunch sometime.' *Yeah right.* 'I'll pay you back soon.' *Oh, sure.* 'Can I have just one minute of your time?' *One minute? Really?*

"Do you ever exaggerate the truth? Tell a story and put an extra spin on it? . . . Do you ever minimize the truth? Confess to a sin less serious than the one you committed? Do you ever twist the truth to make someone else look bad? Have you ever described another person's words or actions without explaining their context and thereby made that person appear stupid or cruel? . . .

"So the only reasonable choice for any of us is to stop lying. Completely. If we have even the slightest tendency to distort the truth—and who of us doesn't—we need to say, 'From this day forward I purpose in my heart, with the help of God, to speak only the truth, always and in every situation for the rest of my life.' Such a commitment will inevitably improve our relationship with God and with everyone else" (Downers Grove, Ill.: InterVarsity, 1998, 86–88).

"The nearly identical Hebrew expression in Isaiah 6:14 for a *breaking of the spirit* suggests that the effect of words on 'morale' is chiefly in mind here, though it can be taken further" (*Proverbs,* 113).

Question 7. The image of a tree of life is found both at the beginning of Scripture (Gen. 2:9) and at the end (Rev. 22:2). Revelation 22:2 gives a good description of the tree. The author of this proverb compares the healing of the tree to the healing of a well-spoken word.

Question 10. Think of a person who is patient. Now think of a person who speaks with a gentle tongue. How are they alike? How does the gentle person demonstrate patience? Why is the patient person inclined to speak gently? These are some of the things to think through as you help the group to respond to this question.

Question 11. Both patience and gentleness (v. 15) are powerful weapons—the one for persuasion and the other for having a strong impact even on those who have hardened themselves against us.

Study 4

BEING GENTLE IN OUR MINISTRY

1 Thessalonians 2:1–12

Purpose: To follow Paul's example by becoming more gentle in our ministry.

Question 1. There will probably be those in your group who come from broken or severely dysfunctional families, who do not have any memories of gentle moments with their parents. It might be difficult for them to emotionally experience the truth of this study. There may be others for whom such memories are so rare that they treasure them. Still others may come from nurturing homes and have many good memories. It may take effort and great sensitivity to move through this question.

Question 2. Paul's visits to Philippi and Thessalonica are described in detail in Acts 16–17. He tells them that they can see for themselves that their visit had not been a failure. They had delivered good content with good results at great risk.

Question 3. "Paul's conduct had been represented in an unfavourable light to the converts whom he had left behind at Thessalonica, and he now defends himself. He and his companions had made no attempt to exploit them or live at their expense; on the contrary, they had shown all gentleness and care towards them. They had worked night and day in order to earn their own living while they were busy preaching the good news and building up the new-born Christian community" *(The New Bible Commentary: Revised,* 1157).

This is a question that should not be slid over. Help the group to look at and discuss Paul's motives in ministry—both what they were (they spoke as people approved by God to be entrusted with the gospel, they were trying to please God) and what they were not (not in error or with impure motives, not trying to trick them, not trying to please men, not using flattery, not for greed, not looking for praise from men). The discussion of this question is the basis for looking at our own ministry in question 4.

"Missionaries, and indeed all Christian witnesses, are peculiarly vulnerable to criticism, and therefore must make all the more effort to live, and to be seen to live, in a way that is not open to criticism. Paul's conduct as a missionary in Thessalonica seems to have been criticized in his absence, apparently by people outside the congregation, and he now defends himself from various possible accusations.

"So many wandering religious and philosophical teachers travelled around the Roman world making what they could out of their hearers, that it was necessary for the missionaries to stress that their motives and methods were quite different from those of the less scrupulous of their rivals. The criticisms and response to them made here can be paralleled in the writings of some of the ancient philosophers who felt that they too were being unjustly accused. Basically the missionaries were charged with exploiting their followers and living at their expense. All their appeal to the new converts were regarded as ways of deceiving them into paying the missionary high respect—and high fees or presents" (*The New Bible Commentary, Revised:* 1279).

Question 4. We all need to examine our motives for ministry and involvement in others' lives. There is a danger, however, if this leads to such intense introspection and self-doubt that we are not able to give to others for fear of wrong motives. A healthy evaluation calls for trusting God, who knows our hearts and will reveal our motives to us as we ask him to. Scripture is the basis of and standard for our motives in ministry.

Question 6. If there are any parents in the group, you might ask them what it means to share their lives with their children. (Or how anyone has seen their parents sharing their lives with them.) You may be surprised at how lively the discussion becomes!

Question 8. Paul was a godly example to the Thessalonians and to us. Yet we also need to observe living examples of the kind of gentleness and care Paul describes. Such people become models and mentors for us, demonstrating in practical ways what it means to serve Christ and others.

Study 5

THE GENTLENESS OF WISDOM

James 3:13–18

Purpose: To contrast God's wisdom with earthly wisdom and to consider how to integrate God's wisdom into our lives.

Question 3. "'The greatest good is wisdom' according to Augustine. Those words would be a fitting summary for the teaching of James on the vital subject of the wisdom from above. James contends that this wisdom is not merely something which is intellectually understandable; it must be demonstrated practically in Christian lifestyle" (Paul A. Cedar, *The Communicator's Commentary: James, 1, 2 Peter, Jude* [Waco, Tex.: Word, 1984], 74).

"The word James uses is *kalos*, 'lovely', and what he speaks of is the loveliness of goodness, the attractiveness of the good life, its wholesomeness and helpfulness, as seen in the Lord's people: a way of life whose goodness is plain to all who see" (Alec Motyer, *The Message of James,* The Bible Speaks Today [Downers Grove, Ill.: InterVarsity, 1985], 128).

Wisdom is something that is not just possessed in someone's head, but is lived out in their life. Humility has to do with how you view yourself in relation to God, to others, and to the future. Do you put others down to build yourself up? Do you feel competent to do good on your own?

According to Webster, humility is "having or showing a consciousness of one's defects or shortcomings; not proud; not self-assertive; modest. Suggests an unassuming character in which there is an absence of pride and assertiveness. Syn. lowly, (an older equivalent) meek, (stresses a mildness and patience of disposition which is not easily stirred to anger or resentment), modest (implies the absence of pretensions, boastfulness, conceit, etc.)" (*Webster's New World Dictionary of the English Language. College Edition* [New York: The World Publishing Company, 1964]).

Question 4. In order to be wise we must be able to admit need. This takes the absence of pride and assertiveness, boastfulness, pretense, and conceit. In a sense, humility is the opposite of control. It is admitting that we cannot control everything and need the help of God and others.

James is writing about the impossibility of living the Christian life by our own resources and then about a spirituality that comes from God. It is only in humility that we can admit that we cannot live the Christian life without the Lord and that we need him.

"James's notion of humility is worth exploring. His term *praytes* is variously translated as 'meekness' and 'gentleness' but 'humility' is much to be preferred. 'Meekness' today connotes a touch of weakness and passivity, which are not at all true in James's requirement of active obedience. 'Gentleness' is appropriate in reference to our relationships with each other but James has a larger concept in mind as humility.

"This Christian virtue of humility is modeled after the ministry of Christ, who served others, sacrificed himself and placed himself wholly at the Father's disposal in perfect trust and obedience.

"This seems to be very much James's own concept of humility, as observed in three applications within his letter. Humility is, first, the teachability by which we are to accept 'humbly' the word of God in 1:21. But James emphasizes there that humbly accepting God's word entails doing the word. Therefore humility is, second, a submissive readiness to do what the word says with deeds done in . . . humility. Third, James shows in our current passage that in humility toward God we will become humble (and gentle) to live at peace with each other. The opposite of humility is an unwillingness to learn and a refusal to yield: the bitter envy and selfish ambition that will result in disorder. For James, humility is a yielding of oneself in ready teachability and responsiveness to God's word, resulting in a good and unselfish life of peace with other people" (George Stulac, *James,* The IVP New Testament Commentary Series [Downers Grove, Ill.: InterVarsity, 1993], 134–35).

Question 7. This is asking the group to be vulnerable and to expose weakness and sin in themselves. It is approached by beginning to look "out there" at the culture before looking and exposing from the inside. An environment of support and safety is needed as well as a commitment to pray with and for each other. You as the leader have an important role in this process.

Question 8. Some translations actually use the word *gentle* in describing this heavenly wisdom. The NIV doesn't, but the synonyms are definitely there and should be discussed thoroughly.

Question 10. Wisdom produces a good harvest (see v. 18). The kind of life and behavior described in this passage tends to reproduce itself. For instance, if peace permeates a local church, there will not be divisiveness. So as you think about people who demonstrate the gentle wisdom described in this passage (question 9), look further to see the "fruit" or results of their lifestyle.

Study 6

GENTLENESS AND POWER

2 Corinthians 10:1–11

Purpose: To understand that our power as Christians comes not from ourselves but from God. This can give hope to those who are gentle not only in action but in temperament.

Question 2. The Corinthians were comparing Paul to the "superapostles" (11:5) who had come to Corinth and were seeking to undermine Paul's authority and ministry. Evidently, these false apostles were eloquent speakers, professionally trained in oratory. They were quite impressive in person, with bold, outgoing personalities. In other words, they were powerful people—although they knew nothing of God's power. In contrast, Paul appeared to be weak, timid, and unskilled in speaking. In their eyes he was like a dog who barks at a distance but whimpers when someone comes near. What they failed to realize was that the power in Paul's ministry came from God, not Paul.

Question 3. In A. W. Tozer's *The Pursuit of God* we find a description that helps us understand why Paul appeals to the Corinthians by the meekness and gentleness of Christ. Tozer writes, "A fairly accurate description of the human race might be furnished for one unacquainted with it by taking the Beatitudes, turning them wrong side out and saying, 'Here is your human race.' For the exact opposite of the virtues in the Beatitudes are in the very qualities which distinguish human life and conduct.

"In the world of men we find nothing approaching the virtues of which Jesus spoke in the opening words of the famous Sermon on the Mount. Instead of poverty of spirit we find the rankest kind of pride; instead of meekness, arrogance; instead of hunger after righteousness we hear men saying 'I am rich and increased with goods and have need of nothing'; instead of mercy we find cruelty; instead of purity of heart, corrupt imagings; instead of peacemakers we find men quarrelsome and resentful; instead of rejoicing in mistreatment we find them fighting back with every weapon at their command" ([Harrisburg, Pa.: Christian Publications, 1982], 109–10).

"Paul introduces this final section of the epistle . . . with the tone of entreaty, and, further, entreaty 'by the meekness and gentleness of Christ'; that is to say, the spirit and example of Christ provide the norm which should govern all Christian conduct, and not least when an occasion may demand firmness and even severity. . . . The whole redemptive act of Christ's coming to suffer and to die was one of self-humiliation, and Christ's followers are logically called upon by Paul to show the same spirit (Phil. 2:5ff.) and to let their gentleness be known to all men (Phil. 4:5)" (Philip Edgcumbe Hughes, *Paul's Second Epistle to the Corinthians*, The New International Commentary on the New Testament [Grand Rapids, Mich.: Eerdmans, 1962], 345).

Question 4. Since the Corinthians were comparing Paul to the "superapostles" in Corinth (see 11:5), it is best to interpret his metaphor of weapons and warfare in those terms. What weapons did the superapostles have in their arsenal? By reading between the lines we can deduce that they were eloquent, personally impressive, bold, and charismatic. There is nothing intrinsically wrong with such qualities. Yet Paul points out that personal power is powerless in the kind of warfare we face as Christians. Even a weak person (or perhaps *especially* a weak person) equipped with God's power is more effective than a strong person who relies on his own power and talents.

"As his warfare is spiritual, so the weapons with which he fights must be those bestowed by the Spirit. Carnal weapons such as human ingenuity, organizing ability, eloquent diatribe, powerful propaganda, or reliance on charm or forcefulness of personality, are all in themselves quite unavailing in the ceaseless task of pulling down the strongholds in which evil is entrenched. Such carnal weapons may win superficial or temporary victories, but it soon becomes evident that evil has not been driven from its fortress. The only weapons adequate for the struggle come from God, and He alone enables them to be effective. The Greek expression, meaning literally 'mighty to God', is translated by AV 'mighty through God', i.e. 'rendered powerful by God'. The Christian will always be fighting a losing battle against temptation if he tries to fight against evil in his own strength. 'Not by might, nor by power, but by my Spirit, saith the Lord of hosts' (Zc. 1v.6)" (R. V. G. Tasker, *The Second Epistle of Paul to the Corinthians,* Tyndale New Testament Commentaries [Grand Rapids, Mich.: Eerdmans, 1958], 134).

Question 5. We desperately need our eyes opened and our awareness of spiritual warfare heightened. Encourage good discussion on this question. You might be prepared with follow-up questions in the event that they are needed, such as, "How can we distinguish between spiritual and emotional battles? Why are Christians apparently so blind to spiritual warfare? How can we become more aware?"

There are two dangerous ways of looking at spiritual warfare. One is to ignore it and act as if it doesn't exist. The other is to be so caught up in thinking about it that the focus is on the warfare rather than on Christ.

Don't allow this question to take your group off on a tangent and away from the purpose of the study. But do encourage people to look for the spiritual warfare that is all around us.

Question 6. The answer to this question could begin with describing the kind of weapons we do not use. What might be the weapons of the world? Then think about what kinds of things or practices have divine power to demolish strongholds. Some of them are stated in this passage; others are implied.

Question 7. "One of the most astonishing and undeniable arguments for the truth of the Christian religion, and for the omnipotence of God, is the fact that, when faced with the gospel, which is a scandal to the human intellect and folly to proud, unregenerate men, some of the most subtle of human intellects have been led to render submission to the Saviour. Many of the wisest have been content to become fools for Christ's sake, and not a few of the 'freest' of thinkers have surrendered their 'freedom' to become slaves of Him who took upon Himself the form of a servant" (R. G. V. Tasker, *2 Corinthians,* 135).

Question 11. In order to give a sense of closure and completeness to this series of studies, it is important to leave some time for review.

We want to hear from you. Please send your comments about this book to us in care of the address below. Thank you.

ZONDERVAN™

GRAND RAPIDS, MICHIGAN 49530
www.zondervan.com